Waiter! Waiter! Do you have chicken legs?
No sir. I always walk like his.

• • •

What would you call a young shark that sings?
Boy Jaws

• • •

Why does Captain Kirk hear so well?
He's got three ears. A right ear, a left ear, and a final front ear.

• • •

Knock! Knock!
Who's there?
Dismay.
Dismay who?
Dis may come as a shock, but I's your new neighbor.

• • •

Did you hear about the stupid pianist who kept banging his head against the keys?
He was playing by ear.

*Also Published by Ballantine Books:*

1,000 KNOCK KNOCK JOKES FOR KIDS

1,000 JOKES FOR KIDS OF ALL AGES

1,000 MORE JOKES FOR KIDS

OH NO! NOT ANOTHER 1,000 JOKES FOR KIDS

1,000 WHAT'S WHAT JOKES FOR KIDS

# 1,000 CRAZY JOKES FOR KIDS

## by Michael Johnstone

BALLANTINE BOOKS • NEW YORK

Copyright © 1987 by Michael Johnstone

All rights reserved under International and Pan-American Copyright Conventions. Published in the United States of America by Ballantine Books, a division of Random House, Inc., New York.

First published in Great Britain in 1987 by Ward Lock Limited, 8 Clifford Street, London W1X 1RB, an Egmont Company

ISBN 0-345-34694-7

This edition published by arrangement with Ward Lock Ltd.

Manufactured in the United States of America

First Ballantine Books Edition: April 1988
Fourth Printing: June 1989

# Contents

# 1,000
# CRAZY JOKES
# FOR KIDS

# Side splitters

How do you hire a horse?
  Buy it two pairs of stilts.

Why should you never whisper in front of corn?
  Because it has ears.

Where does a sick ship go?
  To the doc.

"Help. Help. My baby's fallen down the well."
  "Hold on. Here's a copy of Dr. Spock."
  "What good's that?"
  "It tells you how to bring up baby."

"Are your parents in, little girl?" asked the man at the door.

"They was, but they's out now," she said.

"Tsk. Tsk. Where's your grammar?"

"In the kitchen doing the washing up."

Why was Santa Claus unemployed?

The elves gave him the sack.

"What's that for?" asked the hotel guest pointing to a pad and paper in the corner of his room.

"That's so you can draw your own bath sir," said the bellboy.

How can you divide seven potatoes among four people?

Mash them.

A man had been telling a very long and very boring joke at a party. "And to cut a long story short . . ." he said. But before he could finish it one of the guests muttered, "Too late!"

Did you hear about the man who sent his beautiful but dumb girlfriend a parrot for Christmas?

It could sing like an angel, recite Shakespeare like an actress, and dance like a ballerina.

"What did you think of the bird?" he asked when next they met.

"It was a bit tough when I took it out of the microwave, so I boiled it with some herbs and it was delicious."

Did you hear about the man who swallowed an unplucked goose?

He felt a little down in the mouth.

How could Noah see in the dark?

He had flood lighting on the Ark.

What did General Custer say when he saw the Indians coming over the hill?

"Here come the Indians."

What did the Italian general say when he saw the GIs coming over the hill?

"Every man for himself."

3

What did the German clockmaker say to the broken clock?

"Ve have vays of making you tock."

Where do Parisians practice shooting?

At the Rifle Tower.

Where do sick gnomes go to be cured?

A national elf service hospital.

"Do you have any last wishes before we shoot?" asked the captain of the firing squad.

"Can I sing one final song?" asked the condemned man.

"Sure."

"Thanks. There were a million in the bed and the little one said roll over, roll over. . . ."

When are pavements at their most slippery?

When the rain's dripping.

Why is *Lord of the Rings* compulsive reading?
  Because it's hobbit forming.

What's wet and makes you scream?
  A big dripper.

Did Moses wear a wig?
  We think so, because sometimes he was seen with Aaron, and sometimes not.

How do you stop your neighbor's cat meowing in your front garden?
  Put it in your other neighbor's front garden.

Where do gnomes go to get fit?
  Elf farms.

Did you hear about the miser who found a pair of crutches and broke his legs so he could use them!

5

What's the North wind's favorite game?
  Draughts.




"Look what I've found," said a man to his friend pointing to an aardvark under his arm.
  "I think you should take it to the zoo," said the other.
  "I think you're right," said the first and set off.
  The next day the two met again and the man still had the aardvark.
  "I thought you were taking him to the zoo."
  "I did. We're off to the cinema today."




"I see you're losing your hair."
  "Nonsense. I know exactly where it is—down the bathroom sink."




MAN AT AIRPORT: I'd like this bag to go to Moscow. This one to New York, and this one to Helsinki.
STEWARD: I'm sorry, sir. We can't do that.
MAN: Nonsense. That's what you did the last time I flew with you.

6

"Got anything to eat, lady?" asked the tramp.

"Do you mind eating last week's leftovers?"

"Not at all."

"Good. Come back next week then."

LANDLADY: I charge $10 a night, $5 if you make your own bed.

GUEST: I'll make my own bed.

LANDLADY: Hang on. I'll get you a hammer and nails.

What was the theatrical agent's favorite song?

There's No Business Like Show People.

"I did what you told me and gave my horse petrol for his cold."

"How is he?"

"He died."

"Funny. So did mine when I tried it."

Why are hairdressers fast drivers?

Because they know all the short cuts.

Who stole Little Bo Peep's sheep?
  Her crook.




ANGRY CAR BUYER: You told me this car was rust free.
SALESMAN: It was. I didn't charge you a penny for it.




"Ladies and Gentlemen: Tonight's speaker is the famous circus clown who for years before he retired made a speciality of sticking his right hand into a tiger's mouth. Ladies and Gentlemen, I give you Lefty."




MAN IN BUS LINE: Where will I catch the number 15 bus?
POLICE OFFICER: Right in the back, sir, if you don't step off the road.




MAN IN BUS LINE: How long will the next bus be?
POLICE OFFICER: About eleven yards, same as all the rest.

What did the bald actor say when he thought about buying a wig?

"Toupee or not toupee?"

Why did the sculptor go mad?

Because he lost his marbles.

"And I promised to remember my sister Jean in my will," read the lawyer from the deceased man's will. "Hello, Jean."

Did you hear about the Eskimo who put some oil heaters in his canoe and was surprised when they exploded and set fire to it?

Which only goes to prove that you can't have your kayak and eat it, too.

What does Santa Claus call reindeer?

Wet, sweetie.

There was nothing in the letter that a woman opened one day except a steel link. And the same the next day, and the day after. She asked the postman if he could explain.

"I think you've been getting some chain mail."

Which famous comedian sacked Rome?
   Attila the Fun.

Why is Sylvester Stallone never on time?
   Because he's always chasing Rambo.

Who stole the dog's voice after it had lost it and then got it back?
   The Raiders of the Lost Bark.

Where would you hear Kojak singing?
   On Top of the Cops.

What book did Tarzan write?
   Lord of the Swings.

Which fly makes films?
  Steven Spielbug.


"I think I'll change my name. Everyone laughs at Michael
Burps."
  "What will you change it to?"
  "John, I think."


Which painter always had a very bad cold?
  Vincent Van Cough.


What squeaks as it solves crimes?
  Miami Mice.


What do you call a man whose wife's left him?
  A divorce-he.


And what do you call his wife?
  Sensible.

"What's your name driver?"
   "Nigel, sir."
   "I always call my drivers by their last name."
   "It's Sweetheart, sir."
   "Drive on, Nigel."

Who's skinny, well dressed, and rules the sea?
   The Princess of Whales.

Who barks as she dances?
   Natalia Makarover.

And who growls when he plays tennis?
   John Macenrover.

The Argyll and Southern Highlanders lost every battle they fought, until in desperation the CO sent for a witch to magic them a lucky mascot.

The old hag consulted her spell book, gathered some ingredients together, and boiled them up. As they bubbled she danced round the cauldron chanting the spell.

Suddenly there was a puff of smoke and a huge demon appeared.

From that day on they never lost a battle, which only goes to prove that demons are Argyll's best friend.

Why couldn't the jellyfish swim?
　It set.

Did you hear about the robot who played poker?
　It threw its hand in.

Where do armies live?
　Up the sleevies of your jacket.

What's a nun's favorite song?
　"I Left My Heart with San Franciscans."

Which Scottish poet is hot stuff?
　Burns.

13

Why are kids with Mohican haircuts good at English?

'Cos they like punktuation.

Did you hear about the strong man who fell through the theater floor?

It was just a stage he was going through.

A glamorous blonde was asked by the bank teller to identify herself before he would cash her check.

She rummaged in her handbag, found a mirror, looked at herself in it, and said, "Oh yes. That's me all right."

"I won't be here for long," boasted the man in the train line. "Several big companies are after me."

"CIA? FBI?"

"No. The phone company, the gas company, and the mortgage company."

What would you do if lightning struck the lavatory?

Don't panic because it won't happen again. It was just a flash in the pan.

What dinosaurs eat tortillas?

Tyrannosaurus Mex.

What happened to the dinosaur who stayed out in the rain?

Stegosaur-rust.

What fruits do schoolboys hate?

Dates.

"I don't want a car," said the farmer to the persistent salesman. "I need a new cow."

"You can't ride a cow along Main Street."

"True. But I can't milk a new car, can I?"

"I can't understand how the cat came to have kittens," an old lady said to the vet. "I never let her out and no other cats are allowed near her."

The vet looked at a large tom sitting by the fireside.

"What about him?" he asked.

"Oh, don't be silly," said the woman. "That's her brother."

What did the duvet say to the feather-filled pillow?
  "Let's get down to business."

BARBER: Were you wearing a red muffler when you came in?"
CUSTOMER: No.
BARBER: Oh dear! I've just cut your throat then.

What did the archaeologist say to the Mummy?
  "I dig you."

ROMAN LEGIONNAIRE: Do you know the time?
OFFICER: Yes: it's XXV past VI.

"What's the difference between a gnat and a gnatter-baby?"
  "What's a gnatterbaby?"
  "Nothing. What's a gnatter with you?"

Two men were standing in a bus line when one turned to the other and said, "I had to take my dog to the vet yesterday."

"Why was that?" asked the other.

"It bit my wife."

"Did you have it put to sleep?"

"No. I had its teeth sharpened."

WIFE: There's something preying on my mind.
HUSBAND: Don't worry. It'll soon die of starvation.

"My wife broke her arm pulling some cabbages in the garden yesterday."

"What did you do?"

"I had to open a tin of beans."

BOY: Daddy, there's a man at the door with a beard.
FATHER: Tell him your mother's got one already.

"Did you meet your wife at the airport yesterday?"

"No. I met her in the railway station about ten years ago."

17

WIFE: I've made the chicken soup.
HUSBAND: Why? What harm has it ever done you?


A little boy was doing his homework one evening and turned to his father and said, "Dad, where would I find the Andes?"

"Don't ask me," said his father. "Ask your mother. She puts everything away in this house."


"I always say a prayer before a meal."
"So would I if I cooked like you."


FRED: I've got a bottle of gin for my wife.
ANDY: Sounds like a great bargain to me.

# Monstrous Fun

When do ghosts play tricks on each other?
   On April Ghoul's Day.

How do you make a ghoul float?
   Two scoops of ice cream, a bottle of Coke, and a slice
of ghoul.

What ghost appears in the play *King Lear*?
   The Ghoul.

Where do Australian ghosts go on holiday?
   Lake Eerie.

What's a devil's picket line called?
    A demon—stration.


Where did Dr. Jekyll find his best friend?
    In Hyde Park.


Why did Frankenstein squeeze his girlfriend to death?
    He had a crush on her.


Did you hear about the witch who looked in the mirror?
    It was a shattering experience.


What did the Pharaohs use to keep their babies quiet?
    Egyptian dummies.


What do wizards stop for on the motorway?
    Witch-hikers.

Which ghost won Wimbledon?
   Yvonne Ghoulagong.

A cannibal finished a huge bowlful of soup and turned to his friend and said, "I've had just about a bellyful of my wife."

"I don't know what to do with my wife these days," said a cannibal to his friend.
   "How about currying her," the friend suggested.

CANNIBAL 1: My wife's a tough old bird.
CANNIBAL 2: You should have left her in the oven for at least another half an hour.

What's a vampire's favorite drink?
   A bloody Mary.

What do Chinese cannibals use instead of knives and forks?
   Chap sticks.

Why do cannibals like motorway cafes?
   Because they serve all sorts of drivers in them.


What do ogres use to write with?
   Ball-point men.


What's Dracula's favorite film?
   The Vampire Strikes Back.


What's a witch's favorite drink?
   Tea-he-he.


What do you get when a cannibal tells you to drop in for a meal?
   Pot luck.


What are baby witches good at in school?
   Spelling.

Where do ghosts go on holiday?
   The Ghosta Brava.

What's a ghost's favorite day of the week?
   The one before Saturday, because it's Frightday.

How does a vampire clean his house?
   With a victim cleaner.

What's a ghost's favorite work of art?
   A ghoulage.

What do drunken ghosts drink?
   Methylated spirits.

Where do vampires keep their savings?
   In blood banks.

Did you hear about the vampire who got married?
    He proposed to his girl-fiend.

Did you hear about the skeleton who challenged another to a duel?
    It was called off as neither had the guts to go through with it.

Why don't cannibals eat missionaries?
    Because you can't keep a good man down.

What song does a ghost sing to warn people that he's around?
    "Beware My Ghoulish Heart."

What's a ghost's favorite Beatles' song?
    "The Ghoul on the Hill."

Who's the most important member in a ghost's soccer team?
    The ghoulie.

Which ghost was president of France?
Charles de Ghoul.

What did the polite ghost say to her son?
"Don't spook till you're spooken to."

What ghost is handy in the kitchen.
A recipe spook.

How did Dr. Frankenstein pay the men who built his monster?
On a piece rate.

Who's the fastest witch?
The one that rides on a *vroooooooom* stick.

Which ghost ate too much porridge?
Ghouldilocks.

What should gymnasts do if they find themselves in a haunted house?
   Exorcise.


Did you hear about the sick werewolf?
   He lost his voice, but it's howl right now.


Who mans the ghoul's ship?
   A skeleton crew.


How does a witch-doctor ask a girl to polka with him?
   "Voodoo like to dance with me?"


Did you hear about the Californian hippy vampire?
   He was ghoul man. Real ghoul.


What does the postman take to vampires?
   Fang mail.

What did the vampire sing to the doctor who cured him of amnesia?
    "Fangs for the Memory."


Did you hear about the vampire who died of a broken heart?
    He had loved in vein.


What do romantic vampires do?
    Neck.


What type of people do vampires like?
    O positive people.


What's a vampire's favorite fruit?
    Necktarines.


What does a vampire stand on after taking a shower?
    A bat mat.

What's a vampire's favorite dance?
The Vaults.

Mr. and Mrs. Hill and their three children were on a touring holiday in Transylvania where they stopped for the night in Count Dracula's castle.

During the night, the evil Count sucked the blood out of all of them and put them in coffins in his vaults.

The next night Dracula sat by the organ thundering out loud music, while down in the cellar the poor Hills stirred in their coffins. They made their way up to the organ gallery and when Dracula saw them he said, "Welcome to the vampire club, the next tune is especially for you." And guess what he began to play?

"The Hills Are Alive to the Sound of Music."

What do vampires play poker for?
High stakes.

What's a vampire's favorite dance?
The Fang Tango.

Did you hear about the vampire who was locked up in the asylum?
He went bats.

What do you call a vampire junkie?
  Count Drugula.

What did the vampire call his false teeth?
  A new fangled device.

What's a vampire's favorite love song?
  "How Can I Ignore the Girl Necks Door."

What does a vampire say to the mirror?
  "Terror, Terror on the wall."

What's a vampire's favorite cartoon character?
  Batman.

What did Leslie Crowther say when he was surrounded
by vampires?
  "Come on dawn!"

Did you hear about the vampire that was seen crawling through the desert crying "Blood. Blood!"

What's pink, lives in a sty, and drinks blood?
  A hampire.

What's Count Dracula's New York house called?
  The Vampire State Building.

What's Count Dracula's least favorite song?
  "Vampire's Burning. Vampire's Burning."

Why does Count Dracula like coffee shops?
  He can eat for necks to nothing in them.

What do cannibals eat at parties?
  Buttered host.

What did the cannibal say when he came home one night and found his wife chopping up a python and a pygmy.

"Oh no, not snake and pygmy pie again."

What do sick cannibals have for breakfast?

Vitamin bills.

Did you hear about the cannibal who crossed the Atlantic on the Concorde?

He told the waiter to take the menu away and bring him the passenger list.

A reporter was captured by some cannibals in the jungle and taken back to the camp where he was prepared for the chief's supper.

"What do you do in England?" asked the cook as he was about to light the fire.

"I was an editor," said the man.

"Well, look on this as promotion. You'll soon be editor-in-chief."

Why did the cannibal go on a vegeterian diet?

He went off people.

When a plane caught fire over the jungle the pilot ejected and landed in a cannibal's pot. The cannibal turned to his friend and said, "What's this flier doing in my soup?"

Why did the cannibal have a hangover?
 He went to a party and got stewed.

CANNIBAL 1: Do you want some beans on toast?
CANNIBAL 2: Human beans?

Why was the cannibal fined $25 by the judge?
 He was caught poaching.

Did you hear about the cannibal who had chronic indigestion?
 He ate someone who disagreed with him.

There was once a cannibal who decided to join the police. When he was being interviewed, the inspector asked him why he wanted to be a policeman.
 "I want to grill all the suspects," he said.

CANNIBAL 1: Come and have dinner at our hut tonight.
CANNIBAL 2: What are you having?
CANNIBAL 1: Hard-boiled legs.

Why didn't the cannibals cook the monk in the stewpot?
  Because he told them he was a friar.

CANNIBAL 1: I can't find anything to eat.
CANNIBAL 2: But the jungle's full of people.
CANNIBAL 1: Yes, but they're all very unsavory.

Why did the cannibal enjoy eating brains?
  They gave him food for thought.

"I say, I say, I say. Did you hear about the cannibals who captured a scrawny old hunter?"
  "No. I didn't hear about the cannibals who captured a scrawny old hunter."
  "It gave them someone to chew over!"

Did you hear about the cannibal family who were caught spying by the witch-doctor?

They were given a roasting.

CANNIBAL 1: An awful thing happened to my wife's family.
CANNIBAL 2: What's that.
CANNIBAL 1: They used to be so healthy, but they've all gone to pot.

The cannibal priest told his flock to close their eyes and say grace. "For whosoever we are about to eat, may the Lord make us truly thankful."

On another occasion he said, "We thank you, Oh Lord, for our daily dead."

Did you hear about the cannibal who committed suicide?

He got himself into a stew.

# What?

What's the difference between a buffalo and a bison?
 Ever tried to wash your hands in a buffalo?

What's the difference between unlawful and illegal?
 Unlawful is against the law: illegal is a sick bird.

What's the difference between the Eiffel Tower and Joan of Arc?
 One's made of metal: the other's Maid of Orleans.

What's the difference between an insomniac and a butcher?
 One stays awake; the other weights a steak.

What's the difference between a witch and c-a-s-t-s.
   One casts spells and the other spells casts.


What's the difference between Santa Claus and a warm dog.
   Santa Claus wears a red suit. The dog just pants.


What's the difference between an angler and a truant?
   One baits his hooks, the other hates his books.


What would Henry VIII be doing if he were alive today?
   Scratching the lid of his coffin.


What would you give someone who forgot to shake the medicine bottle?
   A trampoline.


What's the youngest branch in the army?
   The infantry.

What's green, sticky, and comes from the valleys?
  A taffy apple.

What's the most expensive soup on the menu?
  24-carrot soup.

What would you use to shine a screw?
  Nail polish.

What did the springboard say to the naughty swimmer?
  "You're for the high jump."

What do policemen have for their lunch?
  Truncheon meat sandwiches.

What do you call a widow with a piano on her head?
  A grand dowager.

What lies on the ground 100 feet in the air?
    A sunbathing centipede.

What game do elephants play in a mini?
    Squash.

What's the cheapest pet to feed?
    A giraffe. When you feed it a little goes a long way.

What did the beef say to the kebab skewer.
    "Spear me. Please spear me."

What do you call a tree that makes things?
    An invent-tree.

What do the citizens of Prague like reading?
    Czech books.

What do misers take from libraries?
  Check books.

What tune do wind instruments play best?
  "There's No Business Like Blow Business."

What did the little boy sing as he poured a bottle of Coke
over his granny's grave?
  "Come alive. You're in the Pepsi generation."

What did the gas meter say to the coin that got stuck?
  "Money's getting very tight these days."

What do computers like for their tea?
  Silicon chips.

What goes woof, woof, tock?
  A watch dog.

What's white and deadly quiet?
  A frozen silence.

What's blue and white and slides up and down tables?
  Wimbledon United.

What's soft, sweet, and white with red marks over it?
  Whipped cream.

What's black when it's clean, and white when it's dirty?
  A blackboard.

What's green, smiles, and sings hymns?
  Lettuce with a gladsome mind.

What's made of ice and shoots down Spitfires?
  A Migloo.

What's got horns, udders, and cuts grass?
    A lawn mooer.

What's green and sings in cages?
    Septic parrots.

What's white and travels down the aisle going "chuff, chuff"?
    A bridal train.

What's brown on the inside, brown on the outside, and hops?
    A kangaroo on rye.

What's green, bitter, and explodes?
    A lime bomb.

What's very quiet and explosive?
    A mime bomb.

What's the sweetest rhythm?
   The sugar beat.


What's 4 yards long, got six legs, and would kill you if it fell out of a tree?
   A billiard table.


What do you call two fat men having a chat?
   A heavy discussion.


What do you call a rich dinosaur?
   A gold-blooded reptile.


What do dinosaurs pay bills with?
   Tyrannosaurus checks.


What tartan do dinosaurs wear?
   Tyrannosaurus checks.

What happened when the bed spread?
    The pillow slipped.

What do Chinese kangaroos eat in Chinese restaurants?
    Hop Suey.

What did the man say when he fell into a vat of beer?
    "That was a bitter experience."

What did he feel like when he surfaced?
    Ale and hearty.

What do cars do at the disco?
    Brake dance.

What do you call two parallel lines of cabbages?
    A dual cabbage way.

What do you call a camel with three humps?
  Humphrey.

What's the best present for a man who's got everything?
  Penicillin.

What's the best way to defeat your opponent?
  Cut off his legs.

What goes "Ha-ha, bonk"?
  Someone laughing his head off.

What song did the monk sing to the nun?
  "If you were the only girl in the world, and I was the
only boy. Nothing!"

What do you call an elf that slurps its food?
  A goblin.

What's a slug's favorite drink?
    Roses' Slime Juice.

What did the miser send to the orphanage as a Christmas donation?
    A couple of orphans.

What can't you have for lunch, breakfast, or tea?
    Supper.

What's the oldest thing at the bottom of the sea?
    Tyrannosaurus-wrecks.

What do angels dance to?
    Soul music.

What do boney people use to open doors?
    Skeleton keys.

What's the most breathless thing on television?
　　The Pink Panter Show.


"What's green in summer, sheds its leaves in winter, and has four pairs of legs?"
　　"I don't know."
　　"Trees."
　　"Trees don't have legs."
　　"I know. But they've all been so easy so far I thought I'd make the last one more difficult for you."

# Medical Madness

PATIENT: Doctor, what do I take for a splitting headache?
DOCTOR: Have you tried glue?

PATIENT: Doctor, my tongue's always sticking out.
DOCTOR: Hold it a second—I've got some stamps to lick.

WIFE: Doctor, my husband thinks he's an elastic band.
DOCTOR: Tell him to snap out of it.

47

PATIENT: Tell me straight, Doctor. What's wrong with me?
DOCTOR: How would you like it? Alphabetically?

PATIENT: Doctor, I think I'm losing my mind.
DOCTOR: Don't worry. You won't miss it.

PATIENT: Doctor, how long can a person live without a brain?
DOCTOR: I give up. How old are you?

PATIENT: How can I live to be a hundred, Doctor?
DOCTOR: Give up smoking. Stop drinking. Don't go out with women. And stop eating meat.
PATIENT: And will I live to be a hundred?
DOCTOR: Maybe not, but it will certainly seem like it.

PATIENT: Doctor, how can I broaden my mind?
DOCTOR: How about a stick of dynamite between your ears?

PATIENT: Doctor, people always ignore me. What can I do about it?
DOCTOR: Next.


RECEPTIONIST: Doctor, the Invisible Man's outside.
DOCTOR: Tell him I can't see him without an appointment.


DOCTOR: I've got some good news and some bad news for you.
PATIENT: Tell me the bad news first, Doctor.
DOCTOR: I'm going to have to amputate your legs.
PATIENT: And what's the good news?
DOCTOR: The man in the next bed wants to buy your shoes.


PATIENT: Doctor, what can you give me for water on the brain?
DOCTOR: A tap on the forehead should help.


PATIENT: Doctor, I'd like to leave my body to science.
DOCTOR: Don't bother. We couldn't find a cure for it.

DOCTOR: Mrs. Jones, you've got acute septicaemia.
MRS. JONES: I didn't come here for compliments; I came for treatment.

DISTRAUGHT PARENT: Doctor, my son's swallowed a 50 cent piece. What shall I do?
DOCTOR: Keep him in bed until you see some change.

PATIENT: Doctor, my husband's broken a leg.
DOCTOR: But I'm a doctor of music.
PATIENT: That's all right. It's a piano leg.

PATIENT 1: I didn't see you in surgery last night. What happened?
PATIENT 2: I wasn't feeling very well.

DOCTOR: And how long have you thought you were a cat?
PATIENT: Ever since I was a little kitten.

DOCTOR: How do you find yourself these days?
PATIENT: Oh I just throw back the blankets and there I am.

PATIENT: My wife thinks she's a bird.
DOCTOR: Why didn't she come here herself.
PATIENT: She doesn't like getting out of her cage.

PATIENT: Doctor, my wife thinks she's a clock.
DOCTOR: Are you sure you haven't been winding her up.

PATIENT: Doctor, what's the fastest way to lose 20 pounds?
DOCTOR: Cut your legs off.

MEDICAL STUDENT: There's something written on this patient's foot.
DOCTOR: That's right. It's a footnote.

PATIENT: Doctor, I keep seeing green Martians before my eyes.
DOCTOR: Have you seen a psychiatrist?
PATIENT: No. Only green Martians.

DENTIST: Do you want the good news or the bad news?
PATIENT: Give me the good news.
DENTIST: Your teeth are quite perfect.
PATIENT: What's the bad news.
DENTIST: Your gums are so bad I'll have to take all your teeth out.

PATIENT: Doctor, I think I'm a pair of curtains.
DOCTOR: Now pull yourself together woman.

PATIENT: I have this desperate urge to paint myself gold all over.
DOCTOR: Don't worry. It's just a gilt complex.

PATIENT: I think I'm a chicken.
DOCTOR: I'd better put you into hospital for a few days.
PATIENT: You can't do that. My family needs the eggs.

PATIENT: Doctor, I think I'm a spoon.
DOCTOR: Stay quiet and don't stir yourself.


PATIENT: My family thinks I'm mad because I like chips.
DOCTOR: Nonsense. I like chips too.
PATIENT: Oh good. You must come and see mine. I've got 3,780.


FIRST TONSIL: Why are you all dolled up?
SECOND TONSIL: I'm being taken out by a surgeon to-night.


DOCTOR: Okay! So you think you're a bird. What do you want me to do?
PATIENT: I want some tweetment.


PATIENT: Doctor, I've got kleptomania.
DOCTOR: If I give you something for it, can I rely on you to take it?

53

PATIENT: My wife sent me because she thinks I've lost my memory.

DOCTOR: When did she say that?

PATIENT: When did she say what?

"I've stopped going to the psychiatrist," said a rich New York lady to her best friend. "He told me this morning that I was in love with my handbag."

"That's ridiculous," her friend agreed.

"I know. I mean, we're very fond of each other, but love?"

PATIENT: I find it difficult to sleep, Doctor.

DOCTOR: Perhaps your bed's too hard.

PATIENT: Oh, I'm all right at night. Its during the day. . . .

NURSE: I bet your wife misses you a lot.

PATIENT: No. Her aim's very good. That's why I'm here.

PATIENT: Doctor, I keep seeing frogs in front of my eyes.

DOCTOR: Don't worry. It's only a hoptical illusion.

OPTICIAN: Can you read the bottom line of the chart?
PATIENT: Read it. I was born there.

Did you hear about the dentist who married the manicurist?
   It didn't last. After a month they were fighting tooth and nail.

OPTICIAN: I think you need strong glasses.
PATIENT: How can you tell without examining me.
OPTICIAN: I knew the minute you walked through the window.

DISTRAUGHT MOTHER: Doctor, my baby's swallowed a bullet.
DOCTOR: Well don't point him at anyone till I get there.

OPTICIAN: I think you could do with a pair of glasses.
PATIENT: I'm wearing glasses.
OPTICIAN: Perhaps I could do with a pair of glasses.

DOCTOR: Don't worry. You'll live to be eighty.
PATIENT: It's my eightieth birthday tomorrow.
DOCTOR: There. What did I tell you?


PATIENT: Doctor, I think that there are two of me.
DOCTOR: Why don't you both sit down and one of you tell me all about it.


DISTRAUGHT MOTHER: Doctor, can a child of ten take my appendix out?
DOCTOR: Of course not.
MOTHER: I thought so. You'd better put it back again Son.


PATIENT: Doctor, I can't sleep.
DOCTOR: Lie at the edge of your bed, and you'll soon drop off.


PATIENT: Doctor, I think I'm a bridge.
DOCTOR: What on earth's come over you?
PATIENT: So far, ten cars, three busses and a truck.

PATIENT: Doctor, my wooden leg's giving me a lot of trouble.
DOCTOR: Why's that?
PATIENT: My wife keeps hitting me over the head with it.


DOCTOR: But what's wrong with your glass eye.
PATIENT: If I can see through it, I'm sure it doesn't fool anyone else either.


PATIENT: Doctor, what can you give me to keep my falling hair in.
DOCTOR: How about a matchbox?


DOCTOR: Would you like the good news or the bad news?
PATIENT: Give me the good news.
DOCTOR: You've only got three weeks to live.
PATIENT: If that's the good news, what's the bad news?
DOCTOR: I should have told you two weeks ago.


PATIENT: I think I'm a slice of bread.
DOCTOR: You'll have to stop loafing around.

PATIENT: Doctor, what's the best way to stop smoking?
DOCTOR: Try to avoid setting fire to yourself.


PATIENT: Doctor, I think I'm a bumblebee.
DOCTOR: Buzz off.

# I say. I say. I say.

"I say. I say. I say. My dustbin's full of roses."
"Well throw them away then."
"I can't. Rose's wearing them."

"I say. I say. I say. Did you hear about the diver who went head first into a vat of blood from 300 yards?"
"Was he all right?"
"Yes, he covered himself in gore."

"I say. I say. I say. Did you hear about the nudist colony surrounded by tins of vegetables?"
"No. I didn't hear about it."
"You couldn't see the nudes for the peas."

"I say. I say. I say. Did you hear about the kindhearted pirate?"

"No. I can't say I have."

"His bark was worse than his bite."

"I say. I say. I say. Have you heard about the plastic surgeon who sat by the fire."

"Yes, he melted."

"I say. I say. I say. My girlfriend's an absolute peach."

"You mean she's got soft skin and is sweet?"

"No. She has a heart of stone."

"I say. I say. I say. What can I do about my flat feet?"

"Have you tried a foot pump?"

"I say. I say. I say. Did you hear about the man who bought a wig and no one knew?"

"Yes. He kept it under his hat."

I say. I say. I say. Did you hear about the man who ate a plutonium sandwich?"

"No. What happened?"

"He got atomic ache."

"I say. I say. I say. Did you hear about the dead angel?"

"You mean the one who died of harp failure."

"I say. I say. I say. Did you hear about the tailor who never made any money, but never lost any either?"

"I suppose his business was sew-sew."

"I say. I say. I say. Why did the fridge salesman go bankrupt?"

"I don't know. But no doubt you're going to tell me."

"Business wasn't so hot."

"I say. I say. I say. Did you hear about the ten ton doughnut?"

"I don't believe there's such a thing as a ten ton doughnut."

"I knew you'd never swallow it."

"I say. I say. I say. Did you hear about the girl who giggled every time she sliced bread."

"Yes. I believe she liked crumby jokes."

"I say. I say. I say. Did you hear about the bald vicar."

"No. What about the bald vicar?"

"No 'airs but lots of graces."

"I say. I say. I say. Did you hear the one about the corn-flakes?"

"No. Tell me."

"I'll only tell you the first part, because it's a cereal."

"I say. I say. I say. My car's in mint condition."

"I know. It's got a hole in the middle."

"I say. I say. I say. I've just swallowed the film in my camera."

"My goodness. I hope it doesn't develop into something serious."

"I say. I say. I say. Did you hear the one about the bed that needed changing?"

"No. Tell me about the bed that needed changing."

"I can't. It hasn't been made up yet.

"I say. I say. I say. I've just been bitten by a snake on my arm."

'Which one?"

"I don't know. One snake looks very much like another one to me."

"I say. I say. I say. What'll I say to the man at the door with the wooden leg?"

"Tell him to hop to it."

"I say. I say. I say. Did you hear about the dating agency for chickens that went bankrupt?"

"Yes. I believe they couldn't make hens meet."

"I say. I say. I say. Did you know it takes a dozen sheep to make a sweater?"

"Really. I didn't know they could knit."

"I say. I say. I say. Did you hear about the two lavatory attendants who got married?"

"Was it a marriage of convenience?"

"I say. I say. I say. How do you make a cheese roll?"

"Have you tried pushing it down a hill?"

"I say. I say. I say. What did the miner's wife say to her husband?"

"I don't know. What did the miner's wife say to her husband?"

"I'll coal you in the morning."

"I say. I say. I say. Why do bees hum?"

"It's because they don't know the words."

"I say. I say. I say. My dog plays me at draughts."

"He must be a very clever dog."

"Not really. He's only beaten me twice tonight."

"I say. I say. I say. I've lost my dog."

"Why don't you put an advertisement in the paper?"

"Don't be silly. Dogs can't read."

"I say. I say. I say. I bet you can't say 'iced ink' five times in quick succession."

"Iced ink. Iced ink. Iced ink. Iced ink. Iced ink."

"I know. Why don't you try a deodorant?"

"I say. I say. I say. Did you hear about the dentist who came down with indigestion?"

"No. How did that happen?"

"He filled himself to bursting point."

"I say. I say. I say. One of my ancestors died at Waterloo."

"Really. King's Hussars?"

"No. WHS bookstall."

"I say. I say. I say. Why are Scottish weddings such tidy affairs?"

"I don't know. Why are Scottish weddings such tidy affairs?"

"Because they tie elastic to the confetti."

"I say. I say. I say. If a buttercup's yellow, what color's a hiccup?"

"I don't know. What color is a hiccup?"

"Burple."

"I say. I say. I say. Why did the lighthouse keeper's marriage end in divorce?"

"I don't know. Why did it end in divorce?"

"It was on the rocks from the beginning."

"I say. I say. I say. Why did the rope-maker's business go bust?"

"I don't know. Why did it go bust?"

"Because all his assets were tied up."

"I say. I say. I say. What did the policeman say to his stomach?"

"I don't know. What did he say to his stomach."

"You're under a vest."

"I say. I say. I say. Did you hear about the photographer who couldn't stop taking pictures?"

"No. Tell me about him."

"He was snap happy."

"I say. I say. I say. Did you hear about the cowardly canary?"

"What about the cowardly canary?"

"He was yellow."

"I say. I say. I say. I gave my wife an antimagnetic, waterproof, shockproof, unbreakable watch for her birthday."

"What happened to it?"

"The dog ate it."

"I say. I say. I say. My wife's sixty-five tomorrow and she hasn't got a gray hair in her head."

"That's amazing."

"Not really. She's as bald as a coot."

"I say. I say. I say. I took my wife to the West Indies for our honeymoon."

"Jamaica?"

"No. It was her idea to go there."


"I say. I say. I say. My wife costs me a fortune."

"Tell her to stop spending money."

"I can't. She's too dear to me."


"I say. I say. I say. I take my dog for a tramp in the woods every day."

"Does your dog enjoy it?"

"Yes. But the tramp's getting a little fed up."


"I say. I say. I say. I've got the cleverest wife in the world."

"I bet she's not as clever as mine. Every time she walks down the street she turns into a shop."


"I say. I say. I say. My wife reminds me of the sea."

"You mean she's wild, romantic, and restless."

"No. She makes me sick."

"I say. I say. I say. My husband's name is George, but I call him treasure."

"Why's that?"

"Because everyone asks me where I dug him up."

"I say. I say. I say. My hamster's got no nose."

"How does it smell?"

"Horrible."

# All Creatures
# Great and Small

Two fleas were running across the top of a packet of soap powder.

"Why are we running so fast?" gasped one.

"Because it says, 'Tear along the dotted line!'"

Why couldn't the butterfly go to the dance?

Because it was a moth ball.

How do you make a glow worm happy?

Cut off its tail. It'll be de-lighted.

If darts fly like arrows, what do fruit flies like?

Bananas.

What do you call a mayfly with a machine gun?
　　Baddy Long Legs.

What creepie crawlies do athletes break?
　　Tapeworms.

Which fly captured the ladybird?
　　The dragon-fly.

Did you hear about the cannibal spider that ate his uncle's wife?
　　He was an aunt-eater.

What do you call a flea that lives in Russia?
　　A Moscow-ito.

Did you hear about the maggot that was shut up in Tutankhamen's Tomb?
　　It had a phar-old time.

What's a budgie's favorite soap opera?
    Coronation Tweet.

What birds spend all their time on their knees?
    Birds of prey.

What bird's good for holes?
    Polly-filla.

Where does a 3 yard canary sleep?
    Anywhere it wants to.

Did you hear about the chicken who wanted to take ballet lessons?
    He wanted to be a hentertainer.

Where do birds meet for coffee?
    In a nest-café.

Did you hear about the trainee woodpecker?
   It was learning the drill.

Why is a sofa like a roast chicken?
   Because they're both full of stuffing.

What do you get if your budgie flies into the blender?
   Shredded Tweet.

What did they call the canary that flew into the pastry dish?
   Tweetie Pie.

Why did the baby turkey bolt down his food?
   Because he was a little gobbler.

What do fish sing to each other?
"Salmon-chanted Evening?"

73

Where do shellfish go to borrow money?
    To the prawn-broker.

Where are whales weighed?
    At the whale-weigh station.

How would you send a message to a shark?
    Drop it a line.

Which fish sit on clouds and play the harp.
    Angel fish.

Where are most fish found?
    Between the head and the tail.

Where did the whale go when it was almost bankrupt?
    He went to see the loan shark.

What's dry on the outside, filled with water, and shoots rockets?

A fish tank.

A frog walked into a library and asked the librarian what he would recommend.

"How about this?" asked the librarian, showing him *Toad of Toad Hall*.

"Reddit. Reddit."

How does a sick sheep feel?

Baah-aahd.

What would happen if bulls could fly?

Apart from the fact you'd always have to carry an umbrella, beef would go up.

What animals eat gas?

Otter mobiles.

Did you hear about the cat that ate some cheese?
  He sat by the mouse hole with bated breath.

What would you call a vulgar ram?
  Very non-ewe.

What dog wears contact lenses?
  A cock-eyed spaniel.

What's got two humps and changes color?
  A camel-ion.

What do rabbits call mobile homes?
  Wheel-burrows.

What do you call an animal that's half parrot and half
tiger?
  Anything it tells you to.

"I shot my dog yesterday."
    "Was he mad."
    "Well, he wasn't exactly happy about it."

What did the beaver say to the log?
    "It's been nice gnawing you."

What do gnus read in the morning?
    Gnus papers.

What did the little porcupine say when it walked into a cactus?
    "Hello Mum."

FIRST DOG: My name's Spot. What's yours?
SECOND DOG: I'm not sure. But I think it's "Fetch."

Why was the little bear so spoiled?
    Its mother pandas to its every whim.

What's the smartest animal in Africa?
   The dandy lion.


What's the cleverest animal in Africa?
   The giraffe. It's got a high level of intelligence.


FIRST BAT: Fancy going out for a bite tonight?
SECOND BAT: No. I think I'll just hang around.


"My cat's at university learning languages."
   "Get him to say something foreign, then."
   "Woof. Woof."


"What family does the aardvark belong to?"
   "I didn't know anyone in the street had one."


Why were animals pleased when the gnus left the jungle?
   'Cos no gnus is good gnus.

What's furry and can see just as well from either end?
    A cat with its eyes shut.


What's gray, weighs 3 pounds and squeaks?
    A mouse that could do with going on a diet.


How do you stop moles from digging in the garden?
    Hide all the trowels.


FIRST DOLPHIN: My owner's the cleverest man on earth.
SECOND DOLPHIN: How come?
FIRST DOLPHIN: I've only been here a week, and every
time I take a leap in the air, he's standing by the pool with
a bucket of fish.


What did he get when Tom locked Jerry in the freezer?
    Mice cubes.


Why did the poor dog chase his tail?
    He was trying to make ends meet.

Why did the lizard go on a diet?
　He weighed too much for his scales.

Why don't lambs like arithmetic?
　Because when they add five and three they get ate.

Why do elephants wear running shoes?
　For jogging, of course.

Why do they wear sand-shoes?
　So they don't sink in the sand.

Why do ostriches bury their heads in the sand?
　To look for elephants that forgot to wear their sand-shoes.

Why are elephants gray?
　So they can't be mistaken for raspberries.

"I'm sorry," said the elephant to the hotel manager. "But I can't pay my bill."

"In that case just pack your trunk and get out."

What's the difference between elephants and boiled potatoes?

You can't mash elephants.

What do you give an elephant with big feet?

Big flippers.

What was the elephant doing up a tree?

It thought it was a squirrel and was looking for nuts.

Why's an elephant big, gray and wrinkly?

Because if it was small, yellow, and feathered it would be a canary.

What would you give a nervous elephant?
  Trunkquillisers.


What do you call a 1-yard high elephant?
  Trunkated.

# Knock! Knock!

Knock! Knock!
Who's there?
Felix.
Felix who?
Felix-tremely cold.


Knock! Knock!
Who's there?
Guinevere.
Guinevere who?
Guinevere going to the cinema?


Knock! Knock!
Who's there?
Ina.
Ina who?
(*Sing*) Ina clear day, you can see forever. . . .

Knock! Knock!
Who's there?
Joan.
Joan who?
Joan rush, will you?

Knock! Knock!
Who's there?
Annette.
Annette who?
Annette Curtains will stop people seeing in.

Knock! Knock!
Who's there?
Wendy.
Wendy who?
Wendy come to lock you up, I won't stop them.

Knock! Knock!
Who's there?
Isabel.
Isabel who?
Isabel working? I've been ringing it for hours.

Knock! Knock!
Who's there?
Ammonia.
Ammonia who?
(Sing) Ammonia bird in a gilded cage . . .


Knock! Knock!
Who's there?
Wayne.
Wayne who?
(Sing) Wayne in a manger, no crib for a bed . . .


Knock! Knock!
Who's there?
Ben.
Ben who?
Ben down and lick my boots.


Knock! Knock!
Who's there?
Dismay.
Dismay who?
Dis may come as a shock, but I's your new neighbor.

Knock! Knock!
Who's there?
Percy.
Percy who?
Percy Verence is the secret of success.


Knock! Knock!
Who's there?
Carol.
Carol who?
Carol go if you switch the ignition on.


Knock! Knock!
Who's there?
Michael.
Michael who?
Mike'll smash your teeth in if you don't open the door.


Knock! Knock!
Who's there?
Smee.
Smee who?
Smee. Your brother.

Knock! Knock!
Who's there?
Juan.
Juan who?
Juance upon a time there were three bears . . .




Knock! Knock!
Who's there?
Juan.
Juan who?
(*Sing*) Juan the red, red robin comes bob, bob, bobbin
along . . .




Knock! Knock!
Who's there?
Avon calling. Your bell's broken.




Knock! Knock!
Who's there?
Germaine.
Germaine who?
Germaine you don't recognize my voice?

Knock! Knock!
Who's there?
Minnie.
Minnie who?
Minnie hands make light work.


Knock! Knock!
Who's there?
Robin.
Robin who?
Robin Banks makes you rich quick.


Knock! Knock!
Who's there?
Juan.
Juan who?
Just Juan of those little things sent to try you.


Knock! Knock!
Who's there?
Ivan.
Ivan who?
Ivan package for you.

Knock! Knock!
Who's there?
Emma.
Emma who?
Emma new neighbor. I just called to introduce myself.


Knock! Knock!
Who's there?
Colin.
Colin who?
Colin and see me next time you're passing.


Knock! Knock!
Who's there?
Adam.
Adam who?
Adam nuisance come to borrow some sugar.


Knock! Knock!
Who's there?
Julian.
Julian who?
Julian and August are popular holiday months.

Knock! Knock!
Who's there?
Albert.
Albert who?
Albert you'll never guess.




Knock! Knock!
Who's there?
Huron.
Huron who?
Huron in five minutes so hurry up.




Knock! Knock!
Who's there?
Barbara.
Barbara who?
(*Sing*) Barbara black sheep . . .




Knock! Knock!
Who's there?
Cereal.
Cereal who?
Cereal cold out here.

Knock! Knock!
Who's there?
Earl.
Earl who?
Earl catch a cold if you don't let me in.


Knock! Knock!
Who's there?
Tick.
Tick who?
Tick 'em up. This is a hold up.


Knock! Knock!
Who's there?
Ivor.
Ivor who?
Ivor awful headache. Can you give me an aspirin?


Knock! Knock!
Who's there?
Ivor.
I've just let you in.
This is another Ivor.
Ivor who?
Ivor you let me in or I'll break the door down.

Knock! Knock!
Who's there?
Olive.
Olive who?
Olive in this house. What are you doing in here?



Knock! Knock!
Who's there?
Luke.
Luke who?
Luke through the peep-hole and you'll see.



Knock! Knock!
Who's there?
Phillip.
Phillip who?
Phillip this form for me will you?



Knock! Knock!
Who's there?
Isabel.
Isabel who?
Isabel necessary on your bicycle?

Knock! Knock!
Who's there?
Wanda.
Wanda who?
Wanda buy a toothbrush.


Knock! Knock!
Who's there?
Beammie.
Beammie who?
Beammie up, Scottie.


Knock! Knock!
Who's there?
Amos.
Amos who?
Amos leave in two minutes, so hurry up.


Knock! Knock!
Who's there?
Alex.
Alex who?
Alex plain later when you let me in.

Knock! Knock!
Who's there?
Will.
Will who?
Will you come out with me tonight?


Knock! Knock!
Who's there?
Yvonne.
Yvonne who?
Yvonne to know how many people live here.

# Just Jokes

There was once an old miser who had played golf with the same ball for twenty-five years until one day he lost it and was forced to buy another. He walked into the local sports shop and said, "Well, here I am again."

What did the golf ball say to the golf club?
    "Come up and tee me sometime."

FOOTBALL PLAYER: If I called you rude names would you send me off?
REF: Of course.
PLAYER: But you can't send me off for thinking them can you?
REF: No.
PLAYER: I think you're a ****** ******

A woman and her baby were trapped in a fire. A fireman saw them standing in a window and cried up, "Throw your baby down. I'll catch him. I'm the fireman's soccer team goalkeeper and I haven't let a ball past me in ten years."

The woman threw her baby down and sure enough the fireman caught him . . . and then bounced him on the ground and kicked him over the street.

What do spoil-sport fruits play?
Gooseberry.

An Irishman went to the races and lost $1,000. He put $500 on one horse and another $500 on the instant replay because he couldn't believe that his horse could lose twice in succession.

An Englishman and a Spaniard were playing golf one day. The Spaniard went into a strong lead until the Englishman lost his temper and shot a hole in Juan.

If athletes get tennis elbow, what do astronauts get?
Missile toe!

There was a sign on the golf course that said, "Please don't pick up lost balls . . . until they stop rolling."

SCHOOL CENTER-FORWARD: I could kick myself for missing that goal sir.
P.T. TEACHER: Don't bother. You'd probably miss.

A nurse noticed a golfer pacing up and down outside the operating room where another golfer who had had a golf ball driven down his throat was being treated.
"Is he a relative of yours?" she asked.
"No," said the golfer. "It's my ball."

An Englishman was about to be shot by a firing squad. The officer-in-charge offered him a last cigarette. The man shook his head. "Thanks very much, but I'm trying to give them up. They're very bad for you, you know."

A man walked up the garden path pulling a large box.
"Are you the Widow Jones?" he asked the woman who came to the front door.
"I'm Mrs. Jones. But I'm not a widow."
"Ah. You haven't seen what I've got in this box."

An old lady tried in vain to teach her parrot to speak. But for twenty years it uttered not a word.

One day it squawked, "I can't eat this cabbage. It's full of insects."

"You can talk!" cried the woman. "Why haven't you said anything for twenty years?"

"There hasn't been anything to complain about until today."



What kind of money do fishermen make?

Net profits.



"Will this bus take me to Regent Street?" a visitor to London asked the conductor.

"Upper or Lower?"

"Oh. All of me, I think."



What happened when the Duke of Wellington gave the order to fire at Waterloo?

Napolean Blownapart.



Where do blind sparrows go for treatment?

The Bird's Eye counter.

Why do legs make good Christmas presents?
    Because they're good stocking fillers.

Two men had just finished laying a carpet and decided to have a cigarette. The packet was nowhere to be found but one of the men spotted a lump in the middle of the carpet.

"Blast!" he thought. "I'm not going to take up all the carpet just for a pack of cigarettes." So he got a hammer and flattened the lump.

Just then the owner of the house came into the room holding the packet of cigarettes. "I think these must be yours," she said. "None of us smoke. And by the way, you haven't seen my pet hamster have you?"

Did you hear about the man who hated Santa?
    He suffered from Claustrophobia.

APPLE 1: You look down in the dumps? What's eating you?
APPLE 2: Worms, I think.

Where did Noah keep the bees?
    In the ark 'ives.

Why did the bald man take up jogging?
    To get some fresh 'air.


Two astronauts went to a disco, but they didn't stay.
They felt it lacked atmosphere.


"I'll take it," said the old man to the shop assistant, pointing to a super train set.
    "I'm sure your grandson will like it, sir," said the assis-
tant.
    "I suppose you're right," sighed the old man. "You'd
better give me two."


"How much is that wig?" asked the bald man.
    "$25 plus tax," said the wig maker.
    "Forget the tacks. I'll use 'air fix."


A large lady walked into a pet shop and said, "I'd like a
kitten for my daughter."
    "I'm sorry, Madam," said the shopkeeper. "We don't
do part exchange here."

"I'd like 100 grams of Acetylsalicyclic acid," said the man to a druggist. "And I'd like it in tablet form."

"You mean you'd like some aspirins, sir."

"That's right. I can never remember the name."

"We serve anything you want," boasted a sign in a restaurant, so one smart Alec went in and ordered roast elephant and chips.

"Certainly, sir," said the waiter and went into the kitchen only to reappear a few minutes later looking very crestfallen.

"No elephant," smirked the smart Alec.

"It's not that sir. We've run out of potatoes."

"Have you got any kittens going cheap?" asked a man in a pet shop.

"No, sir," replied the owner. "All our kittens go 'Meow.'"

"I'd like something cheap and nasty for my mother-in-law's birthday," said the customer.

The assistant thought for a moment and then said, "I've got the very thing, sir."

"What's that?"

"My father-in-law."

"What on earth do you think you're doing?" roared a shop-owner to a man who had walked in and licked all the goods.

The man pointed to a sign and said, "Well, that notice says 'Tongue Sandwiches.'"

"I'll just have some gegs," said the man in a grocer's shop.

"Gegs?" said the grocer.

"That's right. I'm going to make scrambled eggs."

"Six packets of mothballs, please," said an old lady to the chemist.

"But I sold you six packets yesterday."

"I know, but my aim's not very good and I keep missing them."

"How much for a haircut?"

"$3.50." said the barber.

"And how much for a shave?"

"$2 sir."

"Very well, shave my head."

"Have you any vanilla slices left?" A woman asked the baker.

"Yes, madam. Plenty."

"Serves you right for making so many then."

BAKER: These are the best cakes we've had for years, Madam.

CUSTOMER: Then I'd like some you baked more recently please.

WOMAN IN BUTCHER'S SHOP: I want a piece of beef, and make it lean.

BUTCHER: Certainly, madam. Which way?

"Is that the biggest chicken you have?" asked a lady in the butcher's shop.

"No, madam," said the man. He took the bird into the back of the shop and blew it up with his bicycle pump.

"That's better," said the customer, when she saw it. "I'll have them both."

MAN IN IRONMONGER'S SHOP: Have you got long nails?

IRONMONGER: Yes, sir.

MAN: Great. Could you scratch my back for me, please?


MAN IN DRUG STORE: I'd like some rat poison.

DRUGGIST: Sorry, sir, we don't have any. Have you tried Boots?

MAN: Listen, I want to poison them, not kick them to death.


MAN IN BAKER'S SHOP: Have you any broken biscuits?

BAKER: Certainly, sir.

MAN: Well you should be more careful, then, shouldn't you?


"The light's too strong," moaned the artist's model. "And this chair's too hard. I can't stand this dress, my hair's a mess and my lipstick's the wrong color."

"What's your name?" asked the artist.

"Lisa," said the girl.

So the painter called the work "The Moaner Lisa."

CONDUCTOR: Your voice reminds me of pirates.
SINGER: Why's that?
CONDUCTOR: You murder on the High C's.

What's a pig's favorite ballet?
  Swine Lake.

And what ballet do squirrels like?
  The Nutcracker.

SINGER: I throw everything into my work.
CONDUCTOR: Ever thought of digging holes for a living?

"Vincent," said Van Gogh's best friend. "Why did you cut off your ear?"

  "You'll have to speak up," said the artist. "I've just cut off my ear."

What's a composer's favorite game.
  Hyden seek.

SINGER: Do you like music?
CONDUCTOR: Yes. But please finish the song you were singing.


Did you hear about the singer who went to the dentist?
　He gave her a falsetto teeth.


SINGER: My voice is very pure.
CONDUCTOR: I'm not surprised. Whenever you sing you strain it.


Why did Mozart stay in bed all day?
　He was writing sheet music.


SINGER: I'm a natural musician.
CONDUCTOR: Yes. Your tongue's sharp and your feet are flat.


Did you hear about the artist's model who died when the painter threw a sketch at her?
　She had an art attack.

A man walked into a theatrical agent's office, stood on a chair, flapped his arms, and flew twice around the room before landing on the agent's desk.

"How about that then?" he said.

"Sorry," said the agent. "There's no demand for bird impressionists these days."

SINGER: My voice is like a bird's.
CONDUCTOR: Yes. And you've got a brain to match.

Did you hear about the stupid pianist who kept banging his head against the keys?

He was playing by ear.

SINGER: Whenever I sing, the audience always clap their hands.
CONDUCTOR: Over their ears I expect.

Did you hear about the man with the musical moustache?

He fiddled with his whiskers.

What food sings?
A soup opera.

There was once a beautiful fairy who yearned to be a ballet dancer. When she heard that the Royal Ballet were holding auditions in a nearby town, she harnessed 100 white pigeons to her chariot and flew to the theater. The director took one look at her spectacular entrance and told her to go away.

"But why?" she wailed.

"Because I've got enough pigeon-towed dancers in the company already."

A rich woman was sitting by the pool when her husband tripped and fell in. Someone fished him out and cried, "Can anyone here give artificial respiration?"

"What do you mean artificial?" the woman yelled. "We can afford the real thing."

Where would you go to buy jellies?
The Jellycatessen.

How did Moses part the Red Sea.
   With a sea saw.

What did the policeman say to the man with three heads?
   "Hello, hello, hello."

What did the shoe say to the foot?
   "You're having me on."

The monks in an abbey were allowed to speak only once a
year. And every year Brother Ambrose said to the
Abbot how happy he was apart from the fact that there
was no sugar in his tea. And every year the Abbot said
he would do something about it, but he never did.

   After twenty years Brother Ambrose told the Abbot
that he'd decided to leave the Order.

   "Thank goodness for that," said the Abbot. "You've
done nothing but complain since you got here."

What did the pipeline say to the drill?
   "Oil be seeing you."

PARTY HOST: You're John, aren't you. I never forget a face.

GUEST: It's Colin, actually.

HOST: Who said anything about names.

What did the rich man say when his son emigrated to Australia?

"Heir today. Gone tomorrow."

Three men were in court charged with being drunk and disorderly.

"What were you doing?" the judge asked the first one.

"Throwing Smarties in the pond." he said.

"And you?" the judge asked the second.

"I was helping him, sir."

The judge peered at the third and said, "And were you throwing Smarties into the pond or just helping."

"No, sir. I'm John Smarties."

# Silly Rhymes and Loony Limericks

Mary had a little lamb,
Its fleece was quite untainted.
When Old Macdonald had a farm,
The poor old doctor fainted.



Little Miss Muffet,
Sat on her tuffet,
Eating her juicy pink melon.
Along came a spider,
And sat down beside her.
She killed it with spider repellant!



Little Jack Horner
Sat in a corner,
Eating a pie filled with pear.

He stuck in his thumb,
And pulled out a plum,
And said, "What's a plum doing in there."


Mary, Mary, quite contrary,
How does your garden grow?
"I put in some seeds,
And up came some weeds,
With dandelions all in a row."


Lilacs are blue, Dilly, Dilly,
Roses are pale.
When I am king, Dilly, Dilly.
You'll go to jail.


Wee Willie Winkie ran through the town,
Upstairs and downstairs in his nightgown,
Along came a policeman and put him under arrest.
So never go out at night—unless you're fully dressed.


The North wind doth blow
And we shall have snow,
And what will poor Robin do then,

Poor thing?
He'll skate on the lake,
A snowman he'll make,
And probably freeze half to death,
    Poor thing.


Baa Baa Black Sheep,
Have you any wool?
Yes Sir. Yes Sir.
Three bags full.
One for my master,
And one for little Penny,
And one for Widow Applebaum.
So you're not getting any.


Pat a cake, pat a cake, baker's man,
Bake me a cake as fast as you can.
    Get all the ingredients off of the shelf.
"Go away," said the baker. "And make it yourself."


Old Mother Hubbard
Went to the cupboard
To fetch her old dog some cold pie.
But when she got there.
The cupboard was bare.
So it took a bite out of her thigh.

Adam wore a fig leaf,
Eve none at all.
The fun began in Autumn,
When the leaves began to fall.




Little pigeon in the sky,
Dropping things from way up high.
Angry farmer wipes his eye,
Very glad that cows don't fly.




There was a young man from Leek
Who instead of a nose had a beak.
   It grew quite absurd
    Till he looked like a bird.
He migrates at the end of next week.




There was a young man from Brazil
Who always ate more than his fill.
   He thought it no matter
    That his waist line grew fatter,
But he burst. Doesn't that make you ill?

114

There was a young man named Ned
Who had eyes at the back of his head.
   When asked where he's going,
   "I've no way of knowing,
But I know where I've been to," he said.


The bottle of Chanel that Willie sent
Was not liked by his girlfriend, Millicent.
   Her words were so cold,
   They argued, we're told,
Through the silly scent, Willie sent Millicent.


An elephant from hilly Tibet
In his cage one day wouldn't get.
   So his keeper quite near,
   Rammed a hose in its rear,
And invented the first jumbo jet.


There was a young lady from Nantes
Who hated each of her aunts.
   So she buried the lot
   In her vegetable plot,
And grew some remarkable plants.

There was an old man from Peru
Who's wife was making the stew.
    She made a mistake
    And her husband did bake.
So a widow she was. Boo Hoo.


There was a young man called Fisher,
Who was angling for fish in a fissure,
    When a trout with a grin
    Pulled poor Fisher in—
Now they're fishing the fissure for Fisher!


There was a young fellow from Kew
Who's girlfirend said, "I'll be true.
    But please understand
    That along with my hand
The rest of me comes with it, too."


A young man who's as bald as a bat
Spilt hair tonic over the mat.
    It's grown so much higher
    We can't see the fire,
And we think that it's smothered the cat.

There was a young lady from Gloucester
Whose granny and grandfather lost 'er.
   Next day she was found
   In the snow-covered ground,
But they didn't know how to defrost her.


A couple who hailed from Rye
Courted for years side by side.
   He said, "Dear, we've tarried
Why don't we get married?"
   "'Cause no one would have us," she cried.


There once was a man with the mumps
Who was terribly down in the dumps.
   He was frumpy and grumpy
   And jumpy and humpy
Because of his terrible lumps.


A cannibal known as Ned
Ate potato crisps in his bed.
   His mother said, "Sonny,
   It's not very funny.
Why don't you eat people instead?"

A fat lady who lived on the Rhine
Was asked at what hour she would dine.
   She said, "At seven,
   And half past eleven,
With a snack at a quarter to nine."


Wilbur Wright said, "Orville, it's grand,
But there's something I don't understand.
   We've discovered all right
   The secret of flight.
But how do we make this thing land?"


There was an old man from Dunoon
Who ate his soup with his fork,
   For he said, "As I eat
   Neither fowl or flesh
I should finish my supper too early."


There was a young girl from Hyde
Who fell down a hole and died.
   Her unfortunate mother
   Tripped into another,
And now they're interred side by side.

# Waiter! Waiter!

Waiter! Waiter! There's a fly in my soup.
   What do you expect for 50 cents, sir? A beetle?

Waiter! Waiter! There's a beetle in my soup.
   Sorry, sir, we're out of flies today.

Waiter! Waiter! What's this fly doing in my soup?
   The butterfly stroke by the look of it, sir.

Waiter! Waiter! There's a mosquito in my soup.
   Don't worry, sir. Mosquitoes have very small appetites.

Waiter! Waiter! This soup's full of toadstools.
Yes, sir. There wasn't mushroom for anything else.

Waiter! Waiter! There's a fly in my soup.
Not fussy what they eat, are they, sir?

Waiter! Waiter! There's a dead fly in my soup.
Yes, sir, it's the heat that kills them.

Waiter! Waiter! There's a fly in the butter.
Yes, sir. It's a butterfly.

Waiter! Waiter! I'll have some kidleys.
Do you mean kidneys sir?
That's what I said. Didle I?

Waiter! Waiter! This egg's bad!
Don't blame me, sir. I only laid the table.

Waiter! Waiter! This chicken's only got one leg.
　　Perhaps it's been in a fight, sir.
　　In that case bring me the winner.

Waiter! Waiter! There's a fly in my soup.
　　Don't panic, sir. I'll call the ASPCA.

Waiter! Waiter! Do you have chicken legs?
　　No, sir, I always walk like this.

Waiter! Waiter! Do you serve children?
　　Only when there's nothing else in the freezer, sir.

Waiter! Waiter! Do you serve lobster?
　　Bring it in, sir. We're not fussy who we serve here.

How did you find the steak, sir?
　　I moved a mushroom and guess what? There it was.

Waiter! Waiter! Do you have frog's legs?
   No, sir, it's just the way I'm standing.


Waiter! Waiter! There's a fly in my soup.
   Don't worry, sir, the spider in the bread will get it.


Waiter! Waiter! There's nothing worse than an apple with a worm in it.
   Oh, there is, sir—half an apple with a worm in it.


Waiter! Waiter! This salad's frozen solid.
   Yes, sir. It's the iceberg lettuce that does it.


Garcon! Garcon! Il y'a un mouche dans le salade.
   Sorry, sir, I don't speak French.


Waiter! Waiter! There's a bee in my alphabet soup.
   Yes, sir, and I hope there's an A, C, and all the other letters as well.

Waiter! Waiter! This fish is very rude.
  Yes, sir. It doesn't know its place.




Waiter! Waiter! I've just been charged $5 for a slice of toast.
  Yes, sir, it's whole meal bread.




Waiter! Waiter! Do you have crepes Suzette?
  No, sir, and the name's Fred.




Waiter! Waiter! There's a wig in my soup.
  Yes, sir, I thought you asked for hair soup.




Waiter! Waiter! There's a frog on my plate.
  Sorry, sir, it was toad in the hole you ordered wasn't it.




Waiter! Waiter! This chicken's disgusting.
  Yes, sir, you asked for grilled foul, didn't you?

Waiter! Waiter! There's a crocodile in my soup.

Yes, sir, you ordered soup and told me to make it snappy.


Waiter! Waiter! This fish tastes of dog meat.

Yes, sir, it's a Rover sole.


Waiter! Waiter! This tea's not fit for a pig.
Sorry, sir, I'll get you something that is.


Waiter! Waiter! Call me a taxi.

Certainly. Are you ready to order Mr. Taxi.


Waiter! Waiter! Will the band play something for me?

Of course, sir.

Good. Tell them to play Monopoly.


Waiter! Waiter! How long will the sausages be?

About 4 inches, I expect, sir.

Waiter! Waiter! This is the worst service I've ever experienced.

You should have heard the vicar in church on Sunday.

Waiter! Waiter! There are two flies in my soup.

That's all right, sir. Have the extra one on me.

Waiter! Waiter! What's this spider doing in my soup?

Trying to save the fly from drowning by the look of it, sir.

Waiter! Waiter! This coffee tastes like soil.

Yes, sir, it was ground this morning.

More coffee, or tea, sir?

If that was coffee, I'll have tea. If it was tea, I'll have coffee.

Waiter! Waiter! How dare you belch in front of my wife?

Sorry, sir, was it her turn.

Waiter! Waiter! Will the pancakes be long?
   No, sir, I expect they'll be round as usual.


Waiter! Waiter! There's a twig in my soup.
   Sorry, sir, I'll just get the branch manager.

# The Wally Collection

What does a Wally call his pet zebra?
  Spot.

"Wally Airways announce the departure of Flight WA592 to New York. It will take off when the little hand's at three and the big hand's at twelve."

Did you hear about the Wally who rang his school teacher one day to say he couldn't come to school as he'd lost his voice?

Knock! Knock!
  "Who's there?"
  "Wally. Is there anybody in?"

There was a Wally who thought the Order of the Bath was his mother, his father, his sister, and then him!

Some people think that Wallys are very mean. It's not true. It's just a rumor they spread so that no one will ask them for a loan.

The police arrested a Wally once for stealing wallflowers. He claimed that they had planted the evidence on him.

Did you hear about the Wally who thought that radioactivity was an exercise program on the radio?

There was once a Wally who had underfloor central heating put in because he wanted to keep the cellar warm.

Why did the Wally put a knocker on his front door?
    He wanted to be considered for the Nobel Prize.

When Wally heard about the Charge of the Light Brigade, he thought they were talking about his electricity bill.

Did you hear about the Wally who was given a quartz watch?

He thought there were four to the gallon.

How many Wallies does it take to change a light bulb?

Four. One to hold the bulb and three to turn the ladder.

A Wally went for an interview for a job as a refuse collector.

"Have you any experience?" asked the inspector.

"No, sir," said the Wally. "But I'll pick it up as I go along.

What is a Wally?

A partition made by brickies!

Did you hear about the Wally who went missing for three weeks?

He couldn't find a way through the revolving door!

Wally was cooking one day and the recipe said "separate two eggs". So he put one in the kitchen and another in the bathroom.

How do you keep a Wally busy for hours?

Give him a tin of corned beef with "open other end" printed top and bottom!

"Wally. How did you break your leg?"

"I was tap dancing but I fell in the sink."

Why did the Wally plant bird seed?

He wanted to grow canaries.

A Wally who lived in Leeds,
Swallowed a packet of seeds.
    In less than an hour
    His nose was a flower,
And his hair was a big bunch of weeds.

"Wally. How did you break your neck?"

"I was putting some toilet water behind my ears and the seat fell on me!"

*Wally's favorite limerick:*
There was a young man from Dundee
Who was stung on his neck by a wasp.
    When asked to explain
    If he felt any hurt.
    He said, "No, but I'm glad it wasn't a hornet."

Did you hear about the Wally who went for an audition for a part in *Star Trek*?

He went dressed up as a tree, because he wanted to play the Captain's log.

WALLY: Give me a return ticket, please.
TICKET CLERK: Where to?
WALLY: Why, back here, of course.

When Wally heard that the cost of postage stamps was going up from 17¢ to 20¢, he went out and bought as many as he could so that he'd save 3¢ every time he posted a letter.

131

Wally was going across the Forth Bridge on a train and he hadn't bought a ticket. The inspector refused to believe that he'd lost it, but Wally stuck to his story. Eventually the inspector lost his temper, picked up Wally's suitcase and threw it into the river.

"Oh, come on," said Wally. "Just because you don't believe me, there's no need to try and murder my little brother."

JIMMY: I bet I can make you talk like an Indian, Wally.
WALLY: How?
JIMMY: Told you.

When Wally's alarm clock broke he went to bed with curlers in his hair so he would make up curly!

An American tourist fell into the Thames right in front of Wally.

"Drop me a line," he shouted.

"How can I?" asked Wally. "I don't know your address."

A Wally pianist once cried,
"The piano stays locked, though I've tried."
His wife said, "You fool,
   Get a good opening tool,
For all the keys are inside!"



Wally's doorbell rang late one night. He crawled out of bed, groped for the light switch, and opened the door.

"I'm sorry to disturb you at this time of night..." began the girl standing there.

"Oh, that's all right," said Wally. "I had to get up to open the door anyway."



Did you hear about the Wally who had floor to ceiling carpets?

He wanted a mat finish on his walls.



In Roman times, the Wallies once invaded the pitch at the Coliseum because they wanted to get the lion's autograph!



Did you hear about the Wally who tried to cross a sheep with a kangaroo?

He wanted to make woolly jumpers.

What happened when Wally set out to swim the English Channel?

He got halfway across and then turned back because he didn't think he'd make it.

How do you confuse a Wally laborer?

Give him three shovels and tell him to take his pick.

How do you make a Wally burn his ear?

Give him a ring when you know he's doing the ironing.

There was once a Wally who was so mean that when he decided to commit suicide, he broke into his neighbor's house to use his gas cooker!

One Christmas Eve another Wally who was just as mean went outside and fired a pistol in the air. He went back inside and told his kids that Santa Claus had just committed suicide and wouldn't be coming that night.

Why did the Wally eat a nickel?
    His mother told him it was for his lunch.


"Why are you standing on your head, Wally?
    "I'm just turning things over in my mind."


Why did Wally sprinkle sugar all over his pillow?
    He wanted to have sweet dreams.


There was once a Wally who played goalkeeper for the local soccer team and always wore just one glove. When someone asked him why, he explained that it might be warm, but on the other hand, it might be chilly!


Why did Wally take his comb to the dentist?
    Because it had lost all its teeth.


"Why do you have two fried eggs on your head, Wally?
    "Because the boiled ones keep rolling off."

Did you hear about the Wally who was late for school every day? Every time he came to a corner he passed a sign saying GO SLOW—so he did.

A Wally was crawling across the desert when he came across an old Arab.

"Where's the sea?" he gasped.

"About 1,000 miles in that direction."

"In that case," said Wally, "I think I'll stay on the beach."

Did you hear about the Wally who did bird impressions?

He ate worms.

What do you call a Wally with wax in his ears?

Anything you like. He can't hear you.

Why did the Wally wear his shirt in the bath?

Because the label said "Wash and wear."

# Why'scracks.

Why did the star-struck chicken cross the road?
  To see Gregory Peck.


Why did the Roman chicken cross into Switzerland?
  Because it was afraid someone would Caesar.


Why did the dirty chicken cross the road?
  For some foul purpose.


Why did the hedgehog wear spikes to the party?
  Because he was a sharp dresser.

137

Why didn't the skeleton go to the disco?
  It had no body to go with.


Why did the burglar take a shower?
  He wanted to make a clean getaway.


Why did the dumb blonde keep her clothes in the fridge?
  She liked to slip into something cool in the evening.


Why did the potatoes argue all the time?
  They couldn't see eye to eye about anything.


Why are false teeth like stars?
  Because they come out at night.


Why did the schoolgirl take a chisel and hammer to school?
  Because it was breaking up day.

Why do welders work such long hours?
  Because they find their work so riveting.

Why was the dog wearing white sneakers?
  Because his brown boots were at the shoemaker's.

Why does a sheep have a woolly coat?
  Because he'd look stupid in a plastic raincoat.

Why did the nun blindfold herself in the kitchen?
  So she wouldn't see the orange peel.

Why did the silly schoolboy sleep with a banana skin?
  So he could slip out of bed in the morning.

Why did the farmer hit the clock?
  It was self-defense: the clock struck first.

Why are Saturday and Sunday so strong?
  Because the rest are weekdays.

Why didn't anyone take the school bus to school?
  It wouldn't fit through the door.

Why's a psychiatrist like a squirrel?
  Because they're both surrounded by nuts.

Why did the electrician close early on Mondays?
  Because business was very light.

Why are cemeteries in the middle of towns?
  Because they're the dead centers.

Why is an author like a Palace footman?
  They both work for royalty.

Why don't they sell lemonade in Boots?
    Because it leaks through the lace-holes.

"Why does the Prince of Wales wear red, white, and blue braces?"
    "To keep his trousers up?"
    "No. To keep them from falling down."

Why did the doughnut maker retire?
    He was fed up with the hole business.

Why do monks never eat salads?
    Because so many of them are friars.

Why was Mac the Knife so amusing?
    He had a very sharp wit.

Why was the surgeon working on the motorway?
    It needed by-pass surgery.

Why did the arrows shake?
  Because they were all in a quiver.


Why were the firemen called to the flower bed?
  Because it was ablaze with color.


Why are hairdressers so well paid?
  Because they have lots of fringe benefits.


Why is it so trendy to lose your temper?
  Because it's all the rage.


Why did the archaeologist go bankrupt?
  Because his career was in ruins.

# Classroom Capers

TEACHER: Pat. What's a comet?
PAT: It's a star with a tail.
TEACHER: That's right. Jean, can you name one?
JEAN: Rin Tin Tin.

JIM: When I grow up I'm going to be an electrician.
TEACHER: Why do you want to be an electrician, Jim?
JIM: Well, I want a job that gives light relief.

When Mrs. Smith came home one night she was horrified to find her son with his hands round his pet rabbit's throat, shaking it and shouting, "Come on then. What's five and three?"

"Stop it at once," she yelled. "What are you doing?"

"Well, teacher told us that rabbits could multiply quickly. This one can't even add five and three."

143

TEACHER: If you had 20 cents and you asked your granny for another 20 and your grandpa for 30, what would you have John?

JOHN: 20 cents.

TEACHER: You don't know your arithmetic young man.

JOHN: And you don't know my grandparents.


"I'd like to go into the cement business when I leave school," said Billy to the careers master.

"Why do you want to do that?"

"Because mom said I was a great mixer."


TEACHER: If I gave you three rabbits this afternoon and another three tomorrow, how many would you have?

PUPIL: Eight. I've got two already.


TEACHER: Robert. If you don't pay attention, I'll give you a piece of my mind.

ROBERT: Are you sure you can spare it, Miss?


TEACHER: Your little boy almost got a black eye today, but I saved him.

PARENT: Thanks. What happened?

TEACHER: I controlled myself.

A teacher asked one of her pupils why he was crying.

"I washed my canary in Tide and it died," he sobbed.

"But you shouldn't wash your pet in soap powder," said the teacher.

"Oh, it wasn't the soap powder," said the boy. "It was the clothes dryer."

TEACHER: What time do you think Adam was born Sammy?

SAMMY: In the afternoon.

TEACHER: What makes you think that?

SAMMY: Because he was born just before Eve.

PRINCIPAL: Holly, how did you miss school yesterday?

HOLLY: I didn't miss it one little bit, sir.

TEACHER: Jean, what does *trickle* mean?

JEAN: To run slowly.

TEACHER: Good. Annie, what does *anecdote* mean?

ANNIE: It's a short, funny tale.

TEACHER: Well done. Now Rita, give me a sentence with both of these words in it.

RITA: Our dog trickled down the street wagging her anecdote.

TEACHER: Bob, if Captain Cook made five trips round the world and was killed on one of them, which one was it?

BOB: You know I'm no good at history, sir.

TEACHER: Tom, you've got your shoes on the wrong feet.

TOM: They're the only feet I have, sir.

TEACHER: You'll have to do better Bryan. Hard work never killed anyone.

BRYAN: So why should I be the first to try?

TEACHER: David, how do you spell puma?

DAVID: P-O-O-M-A.

TEACHER: The dictionary spells it P-U-M-A.

DAVID: You didn't ask me how the dictionary spells it; you asked me how I spell it.

TEACHER: If I have twenty chips in one hand, and ten in the other, what do I have?

ALEC: Greasy palms.

VOICE ON TELEPHONE: I'm afraid Alice won't be at school today.

PRINCIPAL: Who's calling?

VOICE: It's my mother.

"I'm not going to school today. The teacher's don't like me, the kids call me names, even the caretaker's rude to me."

"Don't be silly. You have to go. I'll give you two good reasons why."

"What are they?"

"One, you're forty years old; and two, you're the principal."

CHEMISTRY TEACHER: Tim, what do you know about nitrates?

TIM: Dad says they're usually twice the days rates!

MICHAEL: When I grow up I'm going to be a ship's carpenter.

TEACHER: Why?

MICHAEL: It'll be plane sailing.

TEACHER: John, I wish you'd pay a little attention.
JOHN: I'm paying as little attention as possible.


What happened when the teacher sat on the drawing pin?
  He got the point.


And what exams do snowmen take?
  Snow levels.


TOM: I'm going to be a baker when I leave school.
TEACHER: Why do you want to be a baker?
TOM: Because they make lots of dough.


ALAN: Miss, I've just had a brilliant idea.
TEACHER: It's probably beginner's luck.


TEACHER: Winston, give me a sentence with the word indisposition in it.
WINSTON: I always play center forward, 'cause I like playing in dis position.

"Why are you late for school, David?" a teacher asked one of his pupils one day.

"I overslept, sir, because I was dreaming of football."

"Why does dreaming of football make you stay in bed?"

"It was 0-0 at half past seven, so they had to play extra time."

GEOGRAPHY TEACHER: Irene, what are the tributaries of the Nile called?
IRENE: Juveniles?

SUNDAY SCHOOL TEACHER: John, I asked everyone who wants to go to Heaven to put their hands up. Why haven't you?
JOHN: 'Cause Mom said I was to go straight home.

MINNIE: Would you punish someone for something she didn't do?
TEACHER: Of course not.
MINNIE: Good, 'cause I haven't done my homework.

"One day my name will be in lights in every theater in the country," said Jenny to her drama teacher.

"I know that you're ambitious, but that's going a bit far," the drama teacher said. "Anyway, how are you going to do it?"

"I'm changing my name to Emergency Exit."

"I'm sorry I'm late, sir, but my father ran over himself last night."

The teacher was very alarmed and asked the breathless boy what had happened.

"He told me to run over the road to get him some cigarettes, but I was too busy doing my homework, so he ran over himself."

TEACHER: Dorothy, who wrote *To a Mouse*?
DOROTHY: I don't know, but I shouldn't think he got an answer."

TEACHER: Ann, if you weigh 80 pounds and you sit in the bath, what happens?
ANNE: The phone rings.

Did you hear about the cross-eyed teacher?
She had no control over her pupils.

TEACHER: Angela, this homework's in your father's handwriting.

ANGELA: Yes, ma'am, I used his pen.

JOHNNIE: When I grow up I'm going to be a printer.

TEACHER: Why do you want to be a printer, Johnnie?"

JOHNNIE: 'Cause Dad says I'm the right type for it.

TEACHER: Fred. Stop fighting. You must learn to give and take.

FRED: I did, sir. I gave him a black eye after he took my sweets.

# What's More?

What do you get if you cross a dog with Concorde?
  A jet setter.

What do you get if you cross a grand piano with a coal digger?
  A flat minor.

What do you get if you cross a hyena with a man-eating tiger?
  I don't know, but if it laughs you'd better join in.

What do you get if you cross a gander with a bramble?
  A gooseberry.

What do you get if you cross a chicken with cement?
    A brick-layer.


What do you get if you cross the Atlantic on the Titanic?
    Very wet.


What do you get if you cross a gun dog with a phone?
    A golden receiver.


What do you get if you cross an Australian dog with a drummer?
    Dingo Starr.


What do you get if you cross a miser with a detective?
    Shylock Holmes.


What do you get if you cross a thrush's leg, a salmon, and a hand?
    Birdsthigh fish fingers.

What do you get if you cross an elephant with a shark?
   Swimming trunks with sharp teeth.

What do you get if you cross an idiot's brain with elastic?
   A stretch of the imagination.

What do you get if you cross a sheepdog with a vegetable?
   A collieflower.

What do you get if you cross ice cubes with an elastoplast?
   A frost aid kit.

What do you get if you cross a stomachache with colored glass?
   A pained glass window.

What do you get if you cross pigs with a lot of grapes?
   A swine glut.

What do you get if you cross a crate of beer with a cat?
  A thirst aid kitty.

What do you get if you cross an abbot with a trout?
  A monkfish.

What do you get if you cross a sheet of glass with indigestion?
  A pain in the gut.

What's higher than an Admiral?
  An Admiral's hat.

What bow can't be tied?
  A rainbow.

What bit of fish doesn't make sense?
  The piece of cod that passeth all understanding.

What was the score when the two ballerinas played tennis?

A tu-tu draw.

What's a punk's national anthem?

Stars and Spikes forever.

What are two-ton raindrops called?

Heavy showers.

What does Tarzan sing at Christmas?

Jungle Bells, Jungle Bells.

What did the sink say to the tap?

"You're such a big drip."

What kind of alarm never goes off?

A false alarm clock.

What did the first potato say to the second potato?
    "If you'd kept your eyes to yourself, we wouldn't be in the soup."

What would you use to shoot wigs?
    An 'airgun.

What fruit is never lonely?
    Pears.

What did the tablecloth say to the table?
    "Don't move. I've got you covered."

What made the Tower of Pisa lean?
    A strict, low-calorie diet.

What barks and kills swimmers?
    Jaws.

What would you call a young shark that sings?
   Boy Jaws.

What do you call a woman who can't stop buying romance novels?
   A heroine addict.

What do you call a man who can't stop buying mats?
   A rug addict.

What's big, hairy, and flies to New York and back in six hours?
   King Concorde.

What's sticky and plays the trumpet?
   Gluey Armstrong.

What steals soap from the bath?
   Robber Ducks.

What was more useful than the invention of the first telephone?

The production of the second telephone.

What did the traffic lights say to the Rolls Royce?

"Listen, big boy. Turn your lights off while I'm changing."

What would you get if you set fire to a nun?

Holy smoke.

What do frogs drink?

Croak!

What did the panda take on its holiday?

Just the bear necessities.

What would you call a skeleton doctor?

"Bones."

What did Moses do with the bones?
He made a skeleton staff to part the Red Sea.

What do Japanese wrestlers have for breakfast?
Kung Food.

What rings and dances at the same time?
The Bell of the Ball.

What film star jumps over trees?
John Treevaulter.

What do you call a judge who's 1 yard tall?
A small thing sent to try us.

What do you call a dog that drinks too much?
A whino.

What do you call 100 strawberries lined up one behind the other?
A strawberry jam.

What would happen if you swallowed an alarm clock?
  Time would pass very slowly.

What are the longest two words in the English language?
  Post Office. Between them they carry millions of letters.

What did the nun say as she crossed the zebra crossing?
  "Now you see me. Now you don't."

What did the baby bee say to the Queen bee.
  "Swarm in here, isn't it?"

What happened to the man who couldn't tell toothpaste from putty?
  His teeth stuck together and his windows fell out.

And what's Mrs. Whitehouse's favorite charity?
  Banned Aid.

# Last Laughs

The judge looked kindly at the woman giving evidence and asked her if she could remember what her husband's last words had been.

"Oh yes, my lord," she sobbed. "He said, 'I wonder how they make a profit selling this red salmon at fifteen cents a can.'"

POLICEMAN: We're looking for a man with a hearing aid.
SUSPECT: Wouldn't a pair of glasses be more useful?

Did you hear about the blacksmith who was being tried in court?

The judge found him guilty of forging.

POLICEMAN: We're looking for a man with one eye.
SUSPECT: Why? Do you only half suspect he's guilty?

A magistrate thundered at the prisoner, "You are charged with driving while under the influence of drink. Are you guilty or not guilty?"

"You tell me, sir," said the accused. "That's what you're paid for, isn't it?"

"Young lady," said the judge. "What gear were you in when you knocked down the nun?"

"Oh, a fur coat, black dress, and red accessories."

JUDGE: Prisoner at the bench, you have been found not guilty of fraud. You are free to leave the court.
PRISONER: Oh good. Can I keep the money as well?

Why was Miss Piggy's boyfriend in court?
    He Kermitted a traffic offence.

POLICEMAN: I'm looking for a man with one eye called Murphy.
SUSPECT: What's his other eye called?

JUDGE: You have been found guilty of the attempted murder of your mother-in-law. But I will only put you on a year's probation.
PRISONER: Thank you your honor.
JUDGE: It's all right. I think you deserve a second chance.

JUDGE: You are accused of driving the wrong way up a one-way street.
IRISHMAN: But, sir, I was only going one way.

POLICEMAN: I'm afraid I shall have to lock you up for the night.
PRISONER: What's the charge?
POLICEMAN: There's no charge, sir. It's all part of the service.

Four prisoners who had shared a cell for so long knew each other's jokes so well that they gave them all numbers rather than tell them.

One day a new prisoner was put in the same cell half way through a joke-telling session.

"89," said the first prisoner and the other three giggled hysterically.

"96," shouted the second and there were hoots of laughter from the other three.

"192," cried the third and the four rolled around the cell floor.

The new inmate thought that he would have a go.

"66," he said. There was silence.

"42," he tried again. Silence.

He turned to one of his cell mates and asked what he was doing wrong.

"It's not the jokes," he was told. "It's the way that you tell them."


A miserable-looking man was sitting in a bar one night.

"Why are you looking so sad?" asked the barman.

"My wife's made me a millionaire." said the man.

"If my wife made me a millionaire, I'd be the happiest man on earth," said the barman.

"Yes, but before I met her I was a multimillionaire."


Did you hear about the one-armed bear that walked into a saloon and said, "I'm looking for ma paw."

A man in a bar slipped off his jacket and slung it over the back of his chair. One of the sleeves hit a woman sitting behind him.

"Watch what you're doing with that sleeve," she complained.

"It's all right," the man said. "There's no 'arm in it."

How did James Bond like his dry martini?

In his mouth like most people.

Two drunks were staggering home along a railway line.

"This is the longest staircase I've ever climbed," moaned one.

"It shertainly ish," slurred his friend. "And the bannister's so low; my back'sh killing me."

A drunk came home one night carrying a pig.

"Where did you pick up that pig?" asked his wife.

"It'sh like thish . . ."

"Shut up," roared his wife. "I wasn't talking to you."

Why did the drunk kick the puppy?

Because it was the heir of the dog that bit him.

A man walked into a pub and said to the pianist, "Do you know your car's on fire outside?"

"No," said the pianist. "But if you hum it, I'll try to follow you."


A drunk walked into a bar and asked the barman if he knew how to make a fruit punch.

"Sure," said the barman. "Give it boxing lessons."


What happened when the barman died?

The police held an inn-quest.


"My father puts people in touch with spirits."

"Is he a spiritualist?"

"No. He runs a pub."


Two simpletons went into a pub and found the snooker table set up for a game.

"Can we have a game?" they asked the barman.

"Sure. It's free."

After an hour neither of them had potted a ball.

"Let's speed things up," said the first idiot.

"How?" asked his friend.

"We'll take the balls out of the frame."

"Does anyone own a large cat with a broad white collar?" shouted a man who ran into a pub.

There was no reply.

"Oh, no. I must have knocked over a nun."

What sea makes you drunk?

The Cider Sea.

A man walked into a bar and ordered a pint of beer and a large Scotch. The barman watched in amazement as the man downed the beer and poured the whisky into his breast pocket.

He ordered another round, then another and another until the barman told him he was too drunk to have any more.

"Step round this side of the bar," said the man to the tall, burly barman.

Just then a little mouse popped out of the man's pocket:

"And bring your cat with you while you're at it." he squeaked.

Why did the priest giggle?

Mass hysteria.

Which holy woman attacked Rome?
    Attila the Nun.


"Is Miss Ellie helping with the lambing?"
    "No boss. But J. R. Ewing."


How do Arabs dance?
    Sheik to sheik.


What's bald, solves murders, and shakes?
    Jelly Savalas.


Which bald actor played James Bond?
    Shorn Connery.


Who sleeps at the bottom of the sea?
    Jack the Kipper.

Which goat was outlawed?
Billy the Kid.

Who's top of the pops in the beehive?
Sting.

Why did the vicar lose weight?
He was on a steeple diet.

How did the burglar get into the house?
Intruder window.

How do you get rid of water on the knee?
Drain-pipe trousers.

"I used to think I was a dog, but the psychiatrist cured me."
"Are you sure?"
"Oh, yes. Just hold my paw and see how firm it is."

170

"I'm sorry, Mrs. Smith, I've just run over your cat. Can I replace it?"

"That all depends on how good you are at catching mice."

A young boy was sitting in the park smoking a cigarette when a policeman came up to him and told him he was too young to smoke.

"Don't be silly," said the boy. "The girl I was out with last night gave it to me and she's younger than me."

The policeman got out his notebook. "And what was her name?"

"Can't remember," said the boy. "That last gin and tonic almost knocked me out."

GRAND LADY: George. Take my dress off.
BUTLER: Er. Certainly, madam.
GRAND LADY: Now, George, take my shoes off.
BUTLER: Er. Certainly Madam.
GRAND LADY: And George . . .
BUTLER: Yes, madam.
GRAND LADY: If you want to keep your job don't wear my clothes again.

Did you hear about the calendar that was given the death sentence?

Its days were numbered.

Why does Captain Kirk hear so well?

He's got three ears. A right ear, a left ear, and a final front ear.

PETSHOP OWNER: That's a very clever bird, sir. If you pull the string on the left leg it sings *God Bless America*. And if you pull the string on its right leg it sings *The Star Spangled Banner*.
CUSTOMER: What happens if I pull both strings at once?
PARROT: It falls off the perch you silly idiot.

"Do you know I dropped my watch in the Seine and it's still running."

"It must be a very expensive watch."

"Not the watch, silly. The river."

How do you make a banana split?

Tell it to buzz off.

"When my grandfather went to the dentist he had all his teeth taken out."

"What did he say when he got home?"

"Never again. Oh, never again."

Did you hear about the new member of Congress who took his seat in the House of Representatives?

The police arrested him and made him take it back.

"Give me a dollar for a cup of tea!" demanded a tramp of a bowler-hatted gentleman.

"Tea doesn't cost that much," snapped the man.

"No, but I thought I'd put all by begs in one ask it."

BRUTUS: What's your favorite movie, Caesar?
JULIUS: ET, Brutus.

Why was Samson so popular?

Because he brought the house down.

Why does an Indian wear feathers?

To keep his wigwam.

There were two Kings in bed. Which one wore the pyjamas?

Mr. King. His wife was wearing a nightdress.

GRANNY: I had to get up early this morning to open the door in my nightie.

ANNIE: That's a funny place to have a door, granny.

Did you hear about the man who ate a candle?
   He only wanted a light snack.

Did you hear about the man with jelly and sponge in one ear and a glass of sherry in the other?
   He was a trifle deaf.

Who's the king of the Kleenex?
   The hankie-chief.

A school leaver who got a job in the local newspaper office was astonished on his first day when a man came into the newsroom and hit everyone on the head with a rolled-up newspaper.

   "Why did he do that?" the lad asked an old reporter.

   "Silly boy," the man said. "Isn't it obvious. He's the 'ead-itor "

A father came home from work one night to find his little boy sitting on the cat, with a pen and paper in his hand.

"Why are you sitting on Spot?" he asked.

"Teacher told us to write an essay on the family pet."

Who's the showiest cartoon character?

Flash Gordon.

Two very snobbish potatoes got married and had a beautiful daughter. When she was twenty-one she asked her mother if she could marry Tom Brokaw.

"Of course not, darling," said the mother. "He's just a common tater."

MOTHER: What are you going to give your baby brother for his birthday, Johnnie?

JOHNNIE: I gave him measles last year. I think I'll try mumps this year.

"Mommy, Mommy, why am I called $6\frac{3}{4}$?"

"Because we drew your name out of a hat."

"Mommy, Mommy, I can't write on an empty stomach."
   "Well, try the table then."

"Mommy, Mommy, why do I always walk round in circles?"
   "Shut up, George, or I'll nail your other foot to the floor."

"Mommy, Mommy, can I go and play with granny?"
   "No, George. You've dug her up twice already this week."

Little Tommy was so well behaved that every time he was good his mother gave him five cents and a pat on the head. By the time he was eighteen he had $2,500 in the bank, but was only 1 yard tall.

"Mommy, Mommy, what's a werewolf?"
   "Shut up, George, and comb your face."

"Mommy, Mommy, I don't want to go to America."

"Stop complaining and keep swimming."

ALISTAIR: Mommy, I'm homesick.
MOMMY: But this is your home.
ALISTAIR: I know: I'm sick of it.

"Mommy, Mommy, why are your hands so lovely and soft?"

"Because the servants do all the housework, darling."

MOMMY: There were two cakes in the larder, Tommy. Now there's only one. Why's that?
TOMMY: I didn't put the light on, so I couldn't see the other one.

"I want my Mommy," cried the young girl who had been taken to a seance for the first time.

The medium went into a deep trance and began to whisper. "Mary. It's me, Mommy. What do you want?"

"I want to know what you're doing there when Daddy told you to sit in the car and keep an eye out for traffic wardens."

"Mommy, Mommy, can I have a glass of water?"

"You've had ten already."

"I know. But my bedroom's on fire."




"Mommy, Mommy, can I go out to play?"

"With your new suit?"

"No. With Andy next door."




MOMMY: Henry stop stretching across the table for a cake. Haven't you got a tongue in your head?

HENRY: Yes Mommy. But it won't reach.




Dear Mommy,

Just to let you know that I was caught smoking in the dorm last night and may be expelled. I put the cigarette in my wastepaper basket and it caught fire and burned the school down. The principal says she'll send the bill for rebuilding to you.

Your loving daughter,

Sally.

P.S. None of this is true, but I have just failed my O levels and thought I would try to put things in perspective for you.

# THEY'RE MORE THAN

# FUNNY...

---

# THEY'RE LAUGH-OUT-LOUD

# HYSTERICAL!

Available at your bookstore or use this coupon.

| | | |
|---|---|---|
| ____1,000 JOKES FOR KIDS OF ALL AGES, Michael Kilgarriff | 33480 | 2.95 |
| ____1,000 KNOCK KNOCK JOKES, Ward Lock, LTD. | 33481 | 2.95 |
| ____1,000 MORE JOKES FOR KIDS OF ALL AGES<br>Michael Kilgarriff | 34034 | 2.95 |
| ____OH NO! NOT ANOTHER 1,000 JOKES FOR KIDS<br>Michael Kilgarriff | 34035 | 2.95 |

 **BALLANTINE MAIL SALES**
Dept. TA, 201 E. 50th St., New York, N.Y. 10022

Please send me the BALLANTINE or DEL REY BOOKS I have checked above. I am enclosing $................(add 50¢ per copy to cover postage and handling). Send check or money order—no cash or C.O.D.'s please. Prices and numbers are subject to change without notice. Valid in U.S. only. All orders are subject to availability of books.

Name_____

Address_____

City_____State_____Zip Code_____

Allow at least 4 weeks for delivery.

TA-160